WITHDRAWN

Other books by Marge Piercy

Fiction

GOING DOWN FAST

DANCE THE EAGLE TO SLEEP

SMALL CHANGES

WOMAN ON THE EDGE OF TIME

Poetry

BREAKING CAMP

HARD LOVING

4-TELLING (*with R. Hershon, E. Jarrett, and D. Lourie*)

TO BE OF USE

LIVING IN THE OPEN

The twelve-spoked wheel flashing

THE TWELVE-

SPOKED WHEEL FLASHING

by Marge Piercy

 ALFRED A. KNOPF   New York   1978

THIS IS A BORZOI BOOK
PUBLISHED BY ALFRED A. KNOPF, INC.

Grateful acknowledgment is made to the following magazines in
which some of the poems in this collection first appeared:

*The American Poetry Review, The Atlantic Monthly, Best Friends,
Big Moon, The Blacksmith, Calyx, Connections, The Feminist Art
Journal, Gravida, Hampton-Sydney Poetry Review, Hanging Loose,
Hard Pressed, The Little Magazine, The Massachusetts Review, The
Minnesota Review, Moondance, Moons and Lion Tailes, One Hundred
Flowers Anthology, Open Places, Out of Sight, Outpost, Painted Bride
Quarterly, Poetry Now, Poets On, Provincetown Magazine, Pulp, Red
Weather, A Room of One's Own, Sojourner, Southern Poetry Review;
Speakout, Speculum, Sunbury, 13th Moon*

Library of Congress Cataloging in Publication Data
Piercy, Marge   The twelve-spoked wheel flashing.   I.   Title.
PS3566.I4T9   813'.5'4   77-15020
ISBN 0-394-42438-7   ISBN 0-394-73488-2 pbk.

FIRST EDITION

For Robert

For Karen   **love**   For Penny

For Woody

.

Contents

The twelve-spoked wheel flashing

The twelve-spoked wheel flashing

A turn of the wheel, I thrust
up with effort pushing, braced and sweating,
then easy over down into sleep, body idle,
and the sweet loamy smell of the earth,
a turn of the twelve-spoked wheel flashing.

I have tried to forge my life whole,
round, integral as the earth spinning.
I have tried to bet my values,
poker played with a tarot deck,
all we hope and fear and struggle for,
where the white chips are the eyes of anguish,
the red the coins of blood paid on the streets
and the blues are all piled by the dealer.
We sit round the table gambling against the house:
the power hidden under the green felt,
the television camera that reads your hand,
the magnetic dice, the transistorized
computer controlled deck that riffles
with the sound of ice
blowing on the wind against glass.

A turn of the wheel: nothing
stays. The redwinged blackbirds implode
into a tree above the salt marsh one
March day piping and chittering
every year, but the banded pet
does not return. The cherry tree begins
to bear this June, a cluster

of sweet black fruit warm on the palm.
The rue died of the winter heaves.
We'll plant a new one. It does not
taste the same, bitter always, but
even in bitterness there are shades,
flavors, subtle essences, discretions
in what sets the teeth on edge.

Down into the mud of pain,
buried, choking, shivering with despair,
the fire gone out in the belly's hearth
and frogs hopping on the floor,
ears sealed with the icy muck,
and the busy shrill cricket of the mad
ego twitching its legs in dry
compulsion all night. Up into the sun
that ripens you like a pear
bronze and golden, the hope that twines
its strands clambering up to the light
and bears fragrant wide blossoms opening
like singing faces.

Turn and turn again and turn,
always rolling on with massive thumps

4

and sudden lurching dives, I am pinned
to the wheel of the seasons,
hot and cold, sober and glad and menacing,
bearing and losing. I turn head high,
head low, my feet brushing the pine boughs,
moss in my ears, my nose gathering
snow, my feet soaked like a tree's
roots. I go rolling on, heads and tails,
turn and turn again and turn,
pinned to the wheel of my choice and choosing still,
stretched on the wheel of the seasons,
learning and forgetting and moving
some part of the way toward
a new and better place, some part
of the way toward dying.

WINTER

Three months exile

1.

Our roses are blooming
with the deep pastels of autumn.
At the top of the bushes buds
furl that will never open.
Here snow skirls in the beams
of my headlights returning
stark late to my cold
corner of nowhere.

Your leg hurts and I cannot
rub it. Both cats
demand to lie on your chest.
In the morning you go alone limping
over our hill to watch the nuthatches
feed and the red-tailed hawk
hunt. You are learning to cook
vegetables in the wok in two
styles of Chinese. I am
learning the taste of loneliness,
water with a bitter tang, alkaline.

2.

I can crawl only so far from my roots
locked into the sand and clay
of our hill knitted secretively
with yours as we stand unlike
as pitch pine and white oak

tangled underground against the force
of the hurricane, the bristling
nor'easter, the sucking
rasp of long drought.

My familiar is the hearth-loving cat
who gallivants tail streaming over the hill,
slithers sneaky through the marsh
sniffing the newsy grasses, who flaunts
singing rich contralto arias
with ear-nicked bar toms rough
and whiskery and sleek slick young
gingery tenors in the bushes,
but comes home complaining always,
murmuring and sighing and rubbing, nobody
but you understands me, nobody
but you, stroke me down,
sweet, yes, home is what you do.

Home is our voices knitted
like roots far down into the sand
and the cold clay and the sweet fresh water,
roots splayed among glacial boulders
bones and oystershells. Home
is our ribs and thighs knitting
year after year and decades
that loose wise knowing
that long warm furry skein.

What the owl sees

Mirror from the twenties
in a gilded frame muting
pleasantly dull, you hung
over the secondhand buffet
in the diningroom
that proved we were practically
middleclass: table with claw
legs, cave of genteel lace.
Underneath I crawled
running my toy car.

In that asbestos box
no room was big enough
to pace more than one stride.
When we shut up we could hear
neighbors in multifamily cages
six feet each side, yelling.
We could smell the liver
and onions frying, we could
hear the tubercular cough
racking an old man's lungs.

When the sun hit your
beveled edge, rainbows would
quiver out to stripe the walls

as sugar candy, pure as
the cry of my hunger.

Now you hang in this rented
space, my only heirloom, over
a radiator, and as I rise
I see my naked body
poised in you like a diver
about to leap.

Your carved frame in childhood
I feared as an owl's head,
eyes of a predator.
You carry in your depths
like mouse bones the starving
blue face of that
unwanted brat. Survival
knocks and hisses.
                    I still
see the wooden owl staring
but beneath I recognize
your sides are gently
curved in and out
female as my own facing
me in you. I smile
at you, at me, at
that battered surviving heiress
of mousebone soup.

War, long war

War, long long war
how you have shaped me
like a prevailing salt wind
from past the curve of the water
stunting and twisting the pines
so they gnarl and stoop crooked
yet stand tough as iron.

War, you old bogey, for how
many years I have lived in your
burning entrails.
How you rotted my sleep,
an ulcer of the mind.

Us became Them and Them
became Us till we bore the flags
of the enemy, whose gentle voices
and inexorable just reason, whose
scale of time and space, thirty years
and village by village, became
our measure of the human,
the vision of strength without armor,
the elephant in the guise of the lily.
Yes, we bore those enemy flags
through the streets of home
where in cameo we fought battles

aimed at stopping battles
there, in the real place
mythical and omnipresent
as the fear of hell
to a believer.

Now our armies too are withdrawn,
the armies of flowers and placards,
the armies of raised fists and rocks,
the handful of real homemade
bombs. The war
that goes on is our war
for our own land. To take it,
to hold it
to form it again new
out of nightmare splitting
open into dream:
half collage of cannibalized machines,
half wailing child.

Five thousand miles

Way past the curve of the earth
in a foreign country
you are sleeping, while it's twilight
here and Venus in its quarter phase
like a silver hook is taken
by a fishy grey cloud over Lake
Michigan. Through the earth
I should burrow to you like a mole.
I should wait for the moon to rise
and bounce off it, radar
to touch your sleeping face.

There in Germany you sleep and here
I walk wakeful and every day
is a calendar square like a prison yard
to pace. Every day is laid on
me and torn off like a bandage
on a slow dripping wound.

I burn with need
of you deep inside like a coal
mine that has caught fire
and smoulders far deep in the rock
away from the healing touch
of the rain, a slow poisonous
fire of wanting and waiting
that melts rocks
to tears of lava.

15

The new novel

I wade into you.
Oh how fat you are.
You want to eat me up.

That is, I guess, how men perceive women:
the way you appear to engulf me
as I invent you.

Through spring and summer and winter
and summer again you
will leach my dreams wan.
I will racket thin nights
through your skeletal rooms
still open to the unfamiliar sky
where ominous green moons
swim through constellations
scratched on my lids.

I will secrete you daily
at length to hang spent
while you crawl from me,
the chrysalis the butterfly abandons.
What remains to me
but to become a caterpillar
yet again:
the best part of me
locked in those
strange paper boxes.

The Greater Grand Rapids lover

In all of Greater Grand Rapids you
are the only one who knows me
the shape of my thighs and my fears
working like yeast
the taste of my laughter
how my teeth chatter
in a cold wind of despairing.

Slowly I evaporate here
drying into a paper scarecrow,
simplified into a scaffolding
of pipes in which a neon
womanfist blinks. I am all
façade and fixed grimaces
like a pinochle deck.

My blood is slowing with
the wide cold brown river.
My frog heart burrows
deep in the mud of the bank.
My hands fold up
and harden on sticks to wait for spring.
My voice flies out over
the stiff grasses of the field
searching and comes back hungry.

Here you have fourteen lovers
and I only one. At home
I have fourteen lovers but here only you
precious as drops of winter sun.
Have you had your vitamin C,

I ask you, take another piece
chicken, let me massage you,
solicitous as an heir
fingering a parchment will.

Curious as snails meeting on a gate
we exchange with soft horns
and wet organs, words and signals,
information, tricks, the history of the soft
flowing foot and the intricate
masonry bower of shell. How the strange
minds twine and glitter and swing
looped in words like a hammock.
How the strange minds joining stand,
charmed snakes glittering
to dance their knowledge.

Round and round I turn
in you, a cat making a bed,
kneading you with my velvet and claws,
butting and nudging and licking,
round and round, and my hair
grows another foot and my eyes
shine gold and red like a carnival.
Then I walk outside and the cold
wind plucks the fur and the shine
from all the branches of my bones.

Skimpy day at the solstice

The whiskey-colored sun
cruises low as a marshhawk
over the dun grass.
Long intricate shadows bar the path.

Then empty intense winter sky.
Dark crouches against the walls of buildings.
The ground sinks under it.
Pale flat lemon sky,
the trees all hooks scratching.

If I could soar I could
prolong daylight on my face.
I could float on the stark
wooden light, levitating
like dried milkweed silk.

Only December and already
my bones beg for sun.
Storms have gnawed the beach
to the cliffs' base. Oaks
in the salty blast clutch ragged
brown leaves, a derelict's
paperbag of sad possessions.

Like the gulls that cross from sea to bay
at sunset screaming, I am hungry.
Among sodden leaves and hay-colored needles
I scavenge for the eye's least
nibble of green.

The Lansing bad penny come again blues

So you turn up like an old
arrest record, so you turn
up like a single boot
after I finally threw the other
away, so you turn up
like a drunken wobbly angel
making your own fierce annunciation
to this battered female
trouble   trouble   trouble.

Tomorrow you go to jail
and tonight you sit before me
brushing me with the gaze
of your eyes burning
and smoky: your eyes that
change, grey
into green into blue,
and that look that never changes.

*Lately I haven't thought
of you every day, lately it hasn't
been as bad,* you say, and
when I laugh, your mouth
calls me cruel.

Ah, you chew your heart
like a steak rare and salty.
When you are cozy in my bed
you twitch with restlessness,

you want to be mirroring your
face in shopwindows in Port
au Prince. When you are gone
a thousand miles you wake up
with the veins of your arm
boring like sirens, and you
want me night and morning
till your belly wrings dry.

I am simple and dogged
as a turtle crossing a road
while you dance jagged epicycles
around me. Now you are
laughing because you know
how to unzip shells. For a few
hours we will both get
just what we want: this is Act
Forty Four in a play
that would be tedious to observers
but for us strict
and necessary as a bullfight,
a duel, the dance of double
suns, twinned stars
whose attraction and repulsion
balance as they inscribe
erratic orbits whose center
is where the other was
or will be.

The breast

The breast comes,
a mountainous sundae of sweet.
The breast goes,
treacherous bird floating aloft with strong white
        osprey wings
on its own selfish currents.

The breast gives
a piss-warm vanilla river
lighting up pleasure in every nerve
like a pinball machine gone haywire.

The breast withdraws
abandoning you to night of a smothering
blanket, hunger crouching
on the belly digging its goad of beak
in the ribs.

The breast has legs that carry it away.
The breast has a belly:
it could turn and suck you dry.
The breast has teeth:
they could tear your flesh.
The breast has eyes that see you:

they could find you wanting.
The breast has arms that reach out to others.
The breast has a mind that will someday
say no more, no more.
The breast runs dry.

How that first sour anger curdles
our quick blood still. How that early
clutching stunts us to misers.
We long to box and be boxed.
We seek to package our lovers
for private consumption until used up.
No response comes rich and creamy enough
to sate ego's hunger, and every
demand back is a summons of impudence
stifling that busy muscle the heart.
Domesticating the wild breast is what
makes a home.

The poet dreams of a nice warm motel

Of course the plane is late
two hours twisting bumpily
over Chicago in a droning grey funk
with the seatbelt sign on.
Either you are met by seven
young Marxists who want to know
at once What Is To Be Done
or one professor who says, What?
You have luggage. But I
parked in the no
parking zone.

Oh, we wouldn't want to put you
up at a motel, we here at
Southwestern Orthodontic Methodist,
we want you to feel homey:
drafty rooms where icicles
drip on your forehead, dorm cubicles
under the belltower where
the bells boom all night
on each quarter hour, rooms in faculty attics
you share with seven crying
babies with measles, rooms two
miles from a bathroom.
                              The bed
is a quarter inch mattress
flung upon springs of upended
razor blades: the mattress

24

is stuffed with fingernail
clippings and the feathers of buzzards.
If you roll over or cough it
sounds like a five car collision.

The mattress is shaped that way
because our pet hippo Sweetie
likes to nap there. It's homey,
isn't it, meaning we're going to keep
you up with instant coffee
until two a.m. discussing why
we at Middle Fork State Teachers College
don't think you are truly great.

You'll love our dog Ogre,
she adores sleeping with guests
especially when she's in heat.
Don't worry, the children
will wake you. (They do.)
In the morning while all
fourteen children (the ones
with the flu and whooping cough
and oh, you haven't had
the mumps—I mean, yet?) assault
you with tomahawks and strawberry
jam, you are asked, oh,
would you like breakfast?
Naturally we never eat
breakfast ourselves, we believe
fasting purifies the system.

Have some cold tofu,
don't mind the mold.

No, we didn't order
your books, that's rampant
commercialism. We will call you
Miz Percy and make a joke about
women's libbers. The mike was run
over by a snowplow.
If we were too busy to put
up posters, we've obtained the
outdoor Greek Amphitheater
where you'll read to me and my wife.
If we blanketed five states
with announcements, we will be astounded
when five hundred cram into
the women's restroom we reserved.

Oh yes, the check will be four
months late. The next hungry poet
will be told, you'll be real comfortable
here, What's-her-name, she wrote that book
The Flying Dyke, she was through last year
and she found it real homey
in the Athens of the West.

Your eyes where I float

Fetched from the airport with my hair unraveled,
the eyes of strangers sticking to my fancy
best coat like dying oysters, self after self
trapped, abandoned in the magician's camera cave
saying fast and slow the responses
shaken from my bones' dice and rambling out
random as teeth on the green baize table
of the media, I am thin
onion skin that shreds in the hand.
The airport wind rattles my slats
where all the words have died
like seedlings deprived of water.
I am glass nobody. Shame steams my windows.

Then on a mattress on a Cambridge floor
while the snow comes down like all those
hasty words I spoke, inside drawn blinds
you fingerpaint me. An eye, a nose,
a mouth, two thighs, red, plum, pale
blue, ivory, puce, black, you layer me,
you build me stroke by stroke.
An embryo I float in your eyes.
Slowly my body swells, the frozen
surface breaks and runs down in sweat.
Our laughter clambers to the ceiling
rampant as a grapevine. How was your trip
you ask, and I say, okay
and stop your mouth so you do not
ask me anything, anything at all
in words.

Nothing you can have

February 28th and here
the first yellow crocuses
lift their cups to the sun,
the raspberries wait to be pruned:
all this morning I have been humming
a theme from Liszt
I cannot have heard since
I played it on the piano
at age seven: the sensuous honey
of melancholy veined
smoky with lust.

At eleven I sucked dreams
like sour lollipops
unsure what I wanted: now
smelly as an old hunting
jacket with blood and sweat
of many rutting seasons,
I still don't
know. It is not what
the how-to books tell
although the inability
to do that well
shrivels the whole thing
like a cold draft
hitting a soufflé.

In my dreaming head
the lovers are dressed
in many layers: they talk
of other things with wit,

seldom of love, they fence.
Always something prevents
that consummation simple
as pissing. Gavottes,
minuets, strategies
complex as a protein molecule
bring them into short elegant
confrontations and whisk
them as quickly apart.

For three years I have
been stolid, content,
hard working, romantic
as a bulldozer moving manure.
February 28th, the sun
tingles, the air enters
my lungs busy as
a minnow flicking and darting.
Yet I droop, head
hanging a too heavy
sunflower, smiling,
sighing, hugging my arms.

At eleven I dreamed
of men who did not exist.
The same now. I know

what I can and cannot have.
The lovers who talk in my mind
are not yet born,
may never be. That dance
is one of equals,
bone by wish.

Spring will come with mud,
and I will slog in boots
to dig and plant my food.
This restlessness will hum
in my blood like a hive
preparing to swarm, and issue
on the still air of summer
buzzing and victorious
to change my life.

Exodus

Out of cattle pen tenements
where the will to live fades out
like a forty watt bulb in the hallway's crotch;
out of streets rampant with proud metal
where men are mice at work
and slavering dogs afterward;
out of beds where women offer up
their only part prized whose name
is an insult and means woman here;
where anxiety yellows the air;
where greed paints over every window;
where defeat private as a worm
gnaws every belly,
we begin our slow halting exodus.
Egypt, you formed me from your clay.
I am a doll baked in your factory ovens,
yet I have risen and walked.

Like the Golem I am makeshift, lumbering.
I rattle and wheeze and my parts
are cannibalized T-birds and sewing machines,
mixers and wheelchairs, hair dryers.
My skin is the papier-mâché of newspapers
cured with the tears of children
pregnant with hunger. My heart
is the stolen engine of an F-111.
My ligaments are knitting needles, hangers
recovered from the bodies of

self-aborted women. My teeth are military
headstones. I am the Golem.
Many breathed rage and hope into my
lungs, their roar
is my voice, their dreams
burning are my fuel.
They say nothing but a desert stretches
beyond, where the skulls of visionaries
are scoured by ants.

We have entered our Thirty Years' War
for a green place called the Country
of the Living. For two generations
we will be walking to a land we must build,
ourselves the bricks, the boards, the bridges,
in every face the map,
in every hand the highway.
We go clanking, stumbling forward, lurching.
Children born in that country
will play in the wreckage of our fears.

SPRING

Archipelago

for Jonny

Seasonal, like a plant
that blooms in a desert.
For months nothing stirs
on baked cracked hills,
discards from a kiln.
Then after the soft rains
you can't see the ground
for the tangle of succulents
lush and twining.
Crowding gold cups gape
wide for the wind
scattering pollen
till the air shimmers.

We meet like dry sticks
scraping. A little sawdust,
claim grinding on claim,
the bang of hard ideas,
the rasp of opposing needs.

We meet like travelers
on an escalator in a busy
terminal, one riding up
while the other is lowered.
They set down the luggage
each is carrying and semaphore
wildly.

We meet like angler
and bucking bass and for

a moment before the line
snaps and the hook is
spat out in a cloud
of blood, a baleful
glancing look is exchanged.

We meet like Stanley
and Livingstone deep in the heart
of darkest fantasy, and as
one approaches brooding
on death and the other
on lecture tours and headlines,
the first words are spoken:
Did you pick up the mail?
What, you mean you didn't
bring my pills?

Yet always we do meet
as we grow older and more
ourselves, we meet
flashing in and out
of trouble, we meet
as the decades swell and buckle,
openly in cafés, clandestinely
on corners, at apartments

camped in overnight
scattered through ramshackle cities,
we meet and always
you are one of the friends
I think of in my life.

Yes, sometimes we meet
and it bursts into our own
season, fierce spring just born
butting, the sun young
and standing high and fiery
at the equinox, unscreened
by leaves, the buds still closed
but swelling, the wind strong
and salty. The dead
grass is pushed aside
by new blades coming
and every dusk the spring
peepers chorus joy from popping
throats deep in the marsh.
Season of plowed furrows, at night
the hunting owl, of seeds and mud,
the time of the hard wind
that quickens, the weightless
rasping caress of the wind.

The first salad of March

Thinnings of the rows,
Chinese cabbage, lettuce, sorrel,
cress; nipped ends of herbs
returning, mint and thyme;
violet leaves poking up
in clusters like armies
of teddy bears emerging
ears first from the earth;
the Egyptian onions that multiply
underground; the spears
of garlic shoots. The mixture
huddles, skimpy in the bowl.

The salad explodes in the mouth,
green romancandles.
It is succulent, dainty,
intense. It is crisp
as new money.
It lights up my blood
and urges fur from
the backs of my hands.
I want to roll in leaves
that are still lumps
on twigs. First salad
strong and fierce and plaintive:
love at age five. Spring
makes new the taste of lettuce
fresh as a tear.

Sacramento, Colorado Springs, Geneva, Middlebury

This poem is born from nothing:
several hours' worth. If I were
home, how the bakery fragrance of the day
would fill my head, how the minutes
would nibble my fingers, how
the phone would roar like an express
train through my thoughts scattering
them, leaving some dead on the tracks,
how the loves that grow out of my belly
would wave their fronds demanding
water, demanding wine, demanding blood
on their deep hard twisting roots,
how the little needs of the moment
would settle, mosquitoes on my arms,
how the tulips would sing to the morning
sun in voices of silk
bells, how my cats would twine
at my legs, how my bed would crouch
at evening like a velvet shoe,
how we would wait to wear each other
and dance.

       This emptiness
drains me hollow as a glass. Why doesn't
anyone here love me right now?
Why isn't someone at the door
to take me walking? Where's the bathroom?
Where's the coffee? the apples? the
stamps? the friendship opening

like a morning's bright tulips?
I say my poems
on the air and the wind blows them
into you and you eat them or
you let them drop like apples
the wind shakes from the tree
and they are born into your blood
or they die on the ground
and the grasses devour them.
But the hours stretch out boring
as expressways to the moon. I am
in a backseat with no map. I am
in a glass fishbowl without water
squinting at the heavy glass that breaks
light into fragments, thorns of pure
color, broken mirror shards of loneliness.
In every town where I don't belong
I collect a little death with my check.

The meaningful exchange

The man talks
the woman listens.

The man is a teapot
with a dark green brew
of troubles.
He pours into the woman.
She carries his sorrows away
sloshing in her belly.

The man swings off lighter.
Sympathy quickens him.
He watches women pass.
He whistles.

The woman lumbers away.
Inside his troubles are
snaking up through her throat.
Her body curls delicately
about them, worrying, nudging
them into some new meaningful shape
squatting now at the center of her life.

How much lighter I feel,
the man says, ready
for business.
How heavy I feel, the woman
says: this must be love.

The market economy

Suppose some peddler offered
you can have a color TV
but your baby will be
born with a crooked spine;
you can have polyvinyl cups
and wash and wear
suits but it will cost
you your left lung
rotted with cancer; suppose
somebody offered you
a frozen precooked dinner
every night for ten years
but at the end
your colon dies
and then you do,
slowly and with much pain.
You get a house in the suburbs
but you work in a new plastics
factory and die at fifty-two
when your kidneys turn off.

But where else will you
work? where else can
you rent but Smog City?
The only houses for sale
are under the yellow sky.
You've been out of work for
a year and they're hiring
at the plastics factory.
Don't read the fine
print, there isn't any.

The love of lettuce

With a pale green curly
lust I gloat over it nestled
there on the wet earth
(oakleaf, buttercrunch, ruby, cos)
like so many nests
waiting for birds
who lay hard boiled eggs.

The first green eyes
of the mustard, the frail
wands of carrots, the fat
thrust of the peas : all
are precious as I kneel
in the mud weeding
and the thinnings go into the salad.

The garden with crooked
wandering rows dug
by the three of us
drunk with sunshine has
an intricate pattern emerging
like the back of a rug.

The tender seedlings
raise their pinheads
with the cap of seed stuck on.
Cruel and smiling with sharp
teeth is the love of lettuce.
You grow out of last year's
composted dinner and you
will end in my hot mouth.

Martha as the Angel Gabriel

Good Martha
you back into town like a tug
small yet massive, hooting, thumping
butting and steering through
the shoals, the temptations, the rocks.
Your politics like a good engine
rattles the decks and churns the wake lively.

Sweet Martha
bulldog butterfly, koala
bear among the eucalyptus
of the Oakland hills,
your heart is shy and your
eyes dart like swallows.

Bereft Martha,
bleeding losses, you are all
you have ever loved in woman after
woman, you yourself, and in your belly
you carry your dead mother,
a pearl of an egg
with a small wet embryo bird
folded inside dreaming of wings.

You are those wings, Martha,
and in you your mother
and your mother's mother climb
to the synagogue roof, standing there

44

black against the sun flapping,
flapping, and take off heavily
as albatrosses, running
to lurch, lumber into the dirty air
and hang unlikely as a boot.
Then off, the big wings
hinging gracefully, higher.
For months at a time, Martha,
for years the albatross
sails the ocean winds and never
bothers to touch land
except to mate.

Agitprop

To come up behind you
and embrace you in the chair
where you sit working
is a guerrilla tactic.
I rush in on the unguarded rear
inflict my affection
and withdraw at once
before the forces of defense can mobilize.
It is unlikely in this manner
that I will seduce you.
However, some force of insurrection
hiding in your rough clothes
might be inspired to rise in revolt.
Thus my attacks can be regarded
as propaganda moves—
promises to the presumably oppressed
of interim relief
and ultimate victory.

Child's Ballads revisited

In the songs handed down
greasy and soft with age, women's strands
run like red wool in the grey
worsted of the braided rug.

"Well met, well met, my own true love,
well met, well met, cried he."
The seductive lover, he will by song's end
mock her in childbirth,
show her the mountains of hell smoking
and strike with his cloven hoof revealed
to sink the wooden ship.

Think of the songs of silkies, heavy men
half seal with tusks and heavy bones and rank coats,
sullen creatures of the cold wet storm
who rise to deposit their baby
in the woman like money in a bank.

Men are the demon other:
courtship wears a human face of caring.
Go off with him and for sure
after marriage or bedding
one morning he turns into the devil,
fangs, hoofs and power,
money in the pocket jangling like spurs,
the engines of his law,

the mills of his fists.
How she will be ground down
to fine white powder, to flour
on that table and bed.

Or ordinary rape. The woman
goes under that rock and never forgets
the weight, the wolf's ready razor,
how it is to be torn
and entered like a deer
brought down for meat.

Like subversive red flannel,
like an ancient pennant of blood
diving and rising in the braided rug
that old harsh wisdom
rubs grating on your fingers:
after surrender the victor
sets the terms.

Expecting

It is a birthday present
that comes in the mail
with no sender you can guess,
only the opaque
company name, that could sell
jewels or long underwear.

It is a dream you almost
remember on waking, and then
in midday it crosses,
a bird flushed from cover
streaking through a clearing
too fast to see the color
but yes, you know it.
It cries now, deep
in the woods.

It is a sunrise flush
warming my breasts
under the shirt, and the constant
effort not to jump up and down
and splatter questions
when your name is said.

It is knowing I do
not know you but I will.

Snow in May

It isn't supposed to happen:
snow on the apple boughs
beside the blossoms, the hills
green and white at once.
Backs steaming, horses
stand in the crusted pasture
switching their tails
in the snow, their broad
flanks like doors of leather
ovens. We lie on a mattress
in the high room with no
heat. Your body chills.
I keep taking parts of you
into my mouth, finny nose,
ears like question marks,
fatfaced toes, raspberry
cock, currant nipples, plum
balls. The snow hangs
sheets over the windows.

My grandmother used to drink
tea holding a sugar cube
between her teeth: hot boiling
strong black tea
from a glass. A gleaming
silver spoon stood up.
Before we make a fire of
our bodies I braid my black
hair and I am Grandmother braiding
her greystreaked chestnut hair
rippling to her waist before
she got into bed with me
to sleep, dead now
half my life. Ice on the palm
of my hand melting,
so cold it burns me.

The window of the woman burning

Woman dancing with hair
on fire, woman writhing in the
cone of orange snakes, flowering
into crackling lithe vines:
Woman
you are not the bound witch
at the stake, whose broiled alive
agonized screams
thrust from charred flesh
darkened Europe in the nine millions.
Woman
you are not the madonna impaled
whose sacrifice of self leaves her
empty and mad as wind,
or whore crucified
studded with nails.

Woman
you are the demon of a fountain of energy
rushing up from the coal hard
memories in the ancient spine,
flickering lights from the furnace in the solar
plexus, lush scents from the reptilian brain,
river that winds up the hypothalamus
with its fibroids of pleasure and pain

twisted and braided like rope,
like the days of our living,
firing the lanterns of the forebrain
till they glow blood red.

You are the fire sprite
that charges leaping thighs,
that whips the supple back on its arc
as deer leap through the ankles:
dance of a woman strong
in beauty that crouches
inside like a cougar in the belly
not in the eyes of others measuring.

You are the icon of woman sexual
in herself like a great forest tree
in flower, liriondendron bearing sweet tulips,
cups of joy and drunkenness.
You drink strength from your dark fierce roots
and you hang at the sun's own fiery breast
and with the green cities of your boughs
you shelter and celebrate
woman, with the cauldrons of your energies
burning red, burning green.

Women of letters

I used to write twenty-two-page-
single-spaced letters to friends,
keeping illegible carbons, not once
in a decade but every week.
Now sometimes I get such letters
from women I don't know, now when
I dictate one-paragraph letters
to lovers.

Somehow I've lost faith in letters,
no longer believe in my biography.
Lost the faith that if I explain everything
love will come in the return mail,
insured, registered, hot
for my signature.

Women dyeing the air with desperation,
women weaving like spiders from the gut
of emptiness, women
swollen with emotion, women with words
piling up in the throat like fallen leaves
to rot there, impacting;

women complaining, telling, retelling
agonies like amber worry beads, sores
like the beads of rosaries, click click,
click click, death, desertion, prison,
neglect, hunger, protestations of

genius and abasement twined
like strands of rotting rope,
I remember, I remember it all.

It is me at fifteen, at nineteen, at
twenty-four or twenty-seven, casting
letters on the face of the dark waters
to float out with the sewage, tearing
bits of small flesh to attract the fluttering birds,
shipping off my dreams, my opinions,
my terrors to people who did not
bother to read them. Who wants to get
a twenty-two-page-single-spaced letter
from a crazy ranting poet-ess housed
in a rotting molar on Wilson Avenue, Chicago,
with a stench of poverty like overripe cheese.
Into the mailslot and out to the super
along with the Sunday funnies
and coffee grounds.

I wrote letters instead of making
speeches, instead of reviewing books,
instead of climbing Mount
Washington, instead of giving poetry
readings at universities, instead of
flying on a business trip to the Coast,
instead of living with the three people who love me,
instead of raising apples and potatoes,

instead of buying a car, instead of
buying a machine gun, instead of
having books I wrote finally published.

Not that they all want to write, except
that print seems to make visible
what others walk through like smog,
the radiation of pain, of need, of identity
screaming like a cat in heat to deaf ears.

After Phyllis wrote *Women and Madness*
they brought the mail in boxes. Boxes upon boxes
like moving day, each full of bloody hanks of hair,
gobbets of flesh, bits of charred skin.
What shall I do with them? she asked us,
drinking gin from a tumbler. *If I answer them
it will take the rest of my life, and how
should I answer them?* Catharine and Martha and I
took each a handful and all evening
we wrote answers, practical, pragmatic (see
your local women's center, clinic, Legal Aid,
send for this booklet, that set of instructions
—plugs, Band-Aids, masking tape).
When we had finished typing, we too got drunk
and still there were more boxes carried up
in the morning, boxes singing
like mad linnets of pain's needle.

Does no one out there listen?
Yet I remember riding with my mother on buses

in Detroit, and I would be so embarrassed I would
tug at her hand, because always
some woman would stare into her face
and begin to tell, click click,
click click, death, desertion, prison,
neglect, hunger, and I think of all the bartenders
drying glasses behind all the bars, and all the psychiatrists
whose clocks tell money by seconds, and all
the letters thrashing like stranded gasping fish
in mailbags everywhere.

Stop writing letters! Stop! We will
come together instead. Each three
will prove that the fourth exists,
will listen, will look, that gift
of open eyes and ears greater than charity.
Let the letters mate like flounder
in the secret bags and their roe ferment.
It is each other only
who can save us with gentle attention
and make us whole.

SUMMER

Ask me for anything else

Patience is dun-colored,
the mousy, the confusing
fall warbler that eats the worms,
the nourishment of beans and whole wheat,
the slow rain the crops
need that grows mold
on the mind.

Watson has patience and muddy
boots, not Holmes with his
cocaine needle. Old dogs
snore their patience.
Cats pace. Big cats
cut patience from the herd
and run it down panting
for hot breakfast.

Patience is a game you play
in a damp chilly cabin
while the river roars
and the path is too soggy
to hike out. Patience
is a tick waiting on a grass
blade for you or your dog.
Patience is the joy
of oysters.

Try me for energy, passion,
hard work, loyalty, hope,

but patience is the spider's
virtue, and I am
the glinting biting fly.

Patience is the library
angel, balancing water
in the air between cups.
I am the fiery one
leaping and gone.
How shall I wait
for you? I wring my hair
dry and the pebbles
of the minutes hit me
in the face. My hands
scrape the air.
I am empty with wanting,
not like a box
but like a tiger's belly.

The pernickety plum tree

The fourth year after we planted it
the Shiro plum tree gave us
two perfect plums
the color of slow clear river
running golden green in the sun,
hue of young grass,
with a fine perfume and savor
sweet and juicy in the mouth.
From the whole tree, graceful
and long limbed, two plums.
Enough to command our attention,
just enough; we each have
half a plum,
justice with a knife.
From a thousand flickering leaves,
from a hundred white blossoms
falling like stars on the path,
two plums: a fable
of highly selective productivity,
or the difficulty of fruition,
or the wisdom of a lazy tree
that we feed, that we water, that we coddle
and pick coppery beetles from,
of our own gullibility
strung along with two plums.

A certain party

An invitation to a cocktail party
fifteen years late
scrawled with a coy notation:
Would love to get together
and talk about any
except one thing.

Is that a skeleton in the corner
used as hat rack? Or is her head
stuffed over the mantel?
But I forget: after the hasty
funeral she was
cremated: her ashes
dispersed on New York smog.

I am a nice chap really,
clever, personable, have a good address
on a tree-lined Village street,
a male roommate, splendid taste
in clothes and objets d'art.
I would not mind collecting a writer,
that is, if your manners have improved.

But they haven't.
You always bought your luck

on the phone to your broker, your forgiveness
at forty an hour from a bald Freudian.

How slowly she bled to death,
her chalky skin becoming
blue as a strangled baby.

You can buy my forgiveness too
a drop at a time
like an icicle melting
of blood,
this time yours.

She died too young, at twenty-three,
long before we had a fighting chance.
Now as I write she sits
on my shoulder, a tiny
unborn monkey chattering
rage.

What is permitted

How beautiful to be let
to stare into your eyes
from inches away, eyes of a shallow
sea with rock on the bottom
volcanic and jagged, rocks that slide
from the pass of scarlet poppies.

How beautiful to be permitted hours
of parentheses inside parentheses,
stories begun with so many details
they cannot end till three a.m.,
the talk stitching with fine silken
embroidery, the questioning with a child's
insistent thump, the angry mind
rooting up assumptions, the quick
pop to a different layer that leaves
me with my breath caught
in my throat like a kite in a tree.

How beautiful to hold you all
of a night, hour after hour,
tides of velvet splashing over,
under, pools of tawny feathers,
flesh that holds sunlight
caught under the skin, to be given
you in me, to move with you, with
you out into the hot

rapids twisting and bobbing
till the river explodes.

How costly to be let into the halls
of your obsessions, buffeted by the moods
that shake you, the floors that
collapse in splinters, the stairways
that run backwards, the afternoons you will
do nothing but stare in the mirror
making faces, the doubts you swing,
bullwhips that threaten to
behead me, the times you walk through
me like fog, the times when you measure
each drop of affection like
an intravenous feeding solution.

What dance is this permitted
by the bearded gnomes of your fears,
two steps backward for each
step forward or is it
the other way round? Hopes
with rosy breast plumage still
build nests in my hair. Pain
puckers you yet I see the strength
there, the woman riding the crimson
lion through a field of flowers
and danger. My friend, of course
I will dance with you, how beautiful
that so much is permitted
when so much is feared.

You ask why sometimes I say stop

You ask why sometimes I say stop
why sometimes I cry no
while I shake with pleasure.
What do I fear, you ask,
why don't I always want to come
and come again to that molten
deep sea center where the nerves
fuse open and the brain
and body shine with a black wordless light
fluorescent and heaving like plankton.

If you turn over the old refuse
of sexual slang, the worn buttons
of language, you find men
talk of spending and women
of dying.

You come in a torrent and ease
into limpness. Pleasure takes me
farther and farther from shore

in a series of breakers, each
towering higher before it
crashes and spills flat.

I am open then as a palm held out,
open as a sunflower, without
crust, without shelter, without
skin, hideless and unhidden.
How can I let you ride
so far into me and not fear?

Helpless as a burning city,
how can I ignore that the extremes
of pleasure are fire storms
that leave a vacuum into which
dangerous feelings (tenderness,
affection, l o v e) may rush
like gale force winds.

For shelter and beyond

For battered women, battered
by the fist of your keeper,
by the nailed boots of the man
drunk on the bottle or the booze of his will,
by the angry man, by the self-pitying man,
by the man kicked by those who can afford
to pass on rage.

For battered women, battered
and bled by hunger, by bills coming
in with the old bills unpaid and the phone
turned off and the children with no
shoes to wear to school.
For battered women, battered
by the rapist in the street,
by the rapist you thought your friend,
by the rapist your uncle, the rapist
in every man who uses women
like something he can wipe himself on.

For battered women, battered
by birthing methods invented for doctors'
profits, with your baby
yanked out of you strapped down,

battered by social workers prying,
battered by jail, battered by divorce
court, battered by electroshock,
battered with drugs that slow your body
and snuff your mind.

For battered women, battered
by insults on the corner and on the job,
by the lack of love, by the loss of love,
by the rancid, garbage abuse that comes
to the aged, by the death of children,
by the death of respect for you
and who you are
battered but alive,
woman ready to give birth again to hope,
ready to midwife hope
for other bleeding women.

Insomnia

Where is that plain door?
That narrow passage,
the hourglass
point where white changes
to soft black: how can
a conscious mind
remember the way through
to embrace its small death?

How beautiful are the waters
of sleep rushing on,
how gratifying is that calm pond
under the fish gape
of the swimming moon.

How full of life the tides
rising and ebbing in every
salty estuary of the flesh,
rich as the sea with neon plankton,
with ancient monsters

sleeking through depths
that flatten and deform,
leaching the ordinary colors.

For nine days I have lost my way,
I have been wandering all night
back corridors, drafty, dreary, ill lit
with doors banging and warnings flashing
tedious as aching molars,
as I search the way through.

I am a bulb left
to burn itself out.
What grumpy clatter
of my forebrain buzzing.
With shame I watch my cats.
Sleep is in the benediction
of the body on the brain
at ease, simple
as breathing.

Going in

Every day alone whittles me.
I go to bed unmated and wake
with a vulture perched on my chest.

I suck my solitude
like a marrowbone, nothing
left but a memory of feasts.

Wait in the silence, wait
empty as a cracked eggshell
for the beating of heavy fast wings

the soft pad of the big cat
the dry grate of scales sliding over rock
the boiling of the waves as he breaches.

I wait for the repressed, the unnamed,
the familiar twisted masks of early
terrors, or what I have always really known

lurks behind the door at night groping
from the corner of my eye, what breaks
through the paper hoop of sleep.

When all of my loves fall from me
like clothing, like the sweet flesh, what
stands but the bones of my childhood

ringed like a treetrunk with hunger
and glut, the tortured gaping
grin of my adolescence homely

as death. Then my bones drop away
like petals, my bones wither
and scatter and still I am waiting

empty as a grey arching sky, waiting
till I fall headlong into my center
the great roaring fiery heart

the crackling terrible furnace of the sun.

Who ever forgives

Coarse rope knotted, fraying
to horsehairs as I pull.
My fingers are raw with picking
the wiry snarl. Where's the way
into the ease of function
when the sleek rope
slips through the hands,
when the pulley spins
and the weight rises?

We are clotted. The fraying
strands chafe us, throttle
us. How we finger
the coarse fibers of pain.

The tangled hairs of our bellies
have thickened to hemp.
We hang in our woven years.
Is there no way through
but to cut loose? to roll free
belittled, lonely
as pulled teeth?
We need the patience
of brown ants to course
the maze of our connection.
How they persist, building
bridges of their bodies.
We are too smart for that.

The summer we almost split

If one night in July one phone call
had never happened, we would now be living
in different houses, the summer I
patented the M. Piercy Total Weight Loss
Through Total Relationship Loss Diet.

It happens to other women, not to me,
the small lies that rot in the bottom
of the basket, the small omissions that rust
through, the slow weight of withdrawal like a change
in the climate that turns farmland to desert.

It happens to other women, not to me,
the solid kitchen plank that breaks suddenly
under your feet and you are falling,
hurtling headfirst in the dark
to wake with a broken hip.

It happens to other women, not to me,
the empty bed, sheets crumpled like a discarded
cigarette pack, the empy man whose love
has gone all at once, empty as
a refrigerator standing in a field.

Well, we came back, didn't we, crawling
and clawing. We came to this place

under a hard clear light and this new
understanding I turn and turn in my hand
like a crystal prism.

For years you have come and gone, loving
and pulling out, taking and running, and now
you claim to have moved in and say you fear
I will leave if I read the fine print
of the quibbling years hidden by your brows.

You think love is a problem you will solve,
a mortgage you will finally pay off. It is you
I have been loving so long and I know where you
have been and how. While you've driven armored
in fantasies, I've walked and slept naked at your side.

The engulfing garden

I can never get away
from you : ten days
out to Portland Oregon
and when I return you bury
me under ninety pounds
of luscious ripe tomatoes.
Eighteen quarts of tomato
juice on the evening of
the third day home, tomato seeds
in my hair, tomato skins
in my teeth, the surfaces
of the kitchen heaped with
tomatoes, tomatoes in buckets,
tomatoes lined up on the window
sills, my hands crisscrossed
with canning cuts, even
my dreams are acid,
running and red. Speak
cruelly and I weep fresh
tomato juice.

Short season

Past timberline alpine
flowers tinge the slope
making clumps some
feet apart in the red
volcanic ash.
Against the rusty scree
the goldfinch-bright stonewort
sprawls, the scarlet
paintbrush, moss campion
at the trickle of the glacier,
the uplifted blue lupine
intense as alcohol flames
wavering in the sun.

Not long ago lava
gushed here killing
everything. The mountain
sleeps fitfully, wakes me
at three in the morning
stirring like a huge
bear in hibernation.
The slowed heart does not
seem to beat but it does.
Spring will come for
the great red bear under
the ice cap, under the sheer crags,
black sails of the buried

ship waiting for the thaw
of fire rising.

Flowers are between disasters.
They happen in the quick
summer, avidly pushing their organs
into the pure sugar rush
of the sun, sucking the rain,
coming in pollen gustily.
But a volcano seen from far
away is a red and gold flower.
After the earthquake,
the explosion, the rivers
of magma, the mountain
is reborn coned
like a perfect breast.

The trouble is I am too small
to take comfort. My eye
stops on the flower, my
life beats in the moment
when the petals unfold,
when my thighs open
and both our bodies
quake and still.

Doors in the wind and the water

Doors open in the mind
and close again like wounds
healing. Doors open in the
mind and close again like
dying fish whose gills fall
finally still. Doors in the mind
open and close like mountains
you see spired white past other
mountains but never reach.

Doors open flashing in the sundarkened wave,
doors in the brown carp pool,
doors in the beard of the waterfall,
doors in the green caverns
of the tree, doors in the eye
of the goat, of the puma,
doors in a hand held up,
doors in the astonished skin.

The self is last summer's
clothes unpacked from suitcases.
The self is your old physics
notebook filled with experiments

you had to fake. A well thumbed
deck where the joker fills in
for the King of Diamonds
and the dog has eaten the Ace
of Spades, but there are
five battered sevens.

Always too at the root tips growing
or dying, dark osmotic exchange
of particles, of energy, of dreams
goes wetly on. The larger mysteries
come to us at morning and evening
crowned with bladderwrack and gull feathers,
wearing the heads of cows, of horned owls,
of our children who are not ours,
of strangers whose faces open
like doors where we enter
or flee.

For Shoshana—Pat Swinton

History falls like rain
on the fields, like hailstones
that break the graceful
fleur de lis spears
of young corn. History falls
like freezing rain
on the small hopes, the
small pleasures of the morning,
the small struggles of a life.
History falls like bombs
scorching the birds on their nests,
burning the big-eyed voles in their tunnels,
the rabbits giving suck
curled in the green grass of June.
Craters pit the smoking fields.
A right hand, a left foot
scattered on the broken road.

History is manufactured like
plastic buckets. History is traded
on the stock exchange and the big
holding corporations
rake off a profit.
History is written to order
like the Sunday funnies. History
is floated like a bond issue
on the fat of banks.

Sometimes time funnels down
to the dripping of water
one drop at a time slow

as the slowest tears right
on the forehead of someone lying
awake remembering, remembering
another year and another face.
Sometimes time stalls in a door
opening, a moment balanced
on a blade of choice when the hand
falters, the face freezes,
and then finally the doors of the will
open or shut
on a yes or a no.

Beyond official history of texts,
of bronze generals,
a history flows of rivers and amoebas,
of the first creeping thing
that shuddered onto the land,
a history of the woman who
tamed corn, a history
of learning and losing, a history
of making good and being had,
of some great green organism
gasping to be free.

Sometimes time funnels down
to a woman who stands in a door
saying no to those who come
with guns and warrants.
Sometimes silence
is a song that carries on the soiled wind
like a flight of geese winging north

to clear cold waters. Sometimes
history that matters is seizing your own,
the old blood clots, the too short dresses,
the anguished masks of failures half
remembered like childhood fevers,
matchboxes from motels off freeways,
snapshots with faces torn out, letters
that said too much or too little,
and saying yes. Yes, I am the person
who acted, who spoke. I grow
from what I was
like a pitch pine after a fire
that pokes up green and bushy shoots
from the charred ground
where its roots spread deep and wide.
I grow from what I was,
more, not less, yes,
in me both egg and stone.
No, I am not a soldier in your
history, I live in my own tale
with others I choose to wake me in the morning,
to sit across the table in the evening,
to wipe my forehead, to touch
my hand, to carry in my throat
like a lullaby that murmurs
no, I do not fear you
and yes, I am not for sale.

Smalley Bar

Anchored a ways off Buoy Rocks the sailboat
bobs jaunty, light, little. We slide
over the side after scraping bottom.
The water up to our waists looks brown
ahead. We wade onto Smalley Bar.
I leave the men clamming and walk
the bar toward shore.

By the time I walk back straight out
from the coast of the wild island the tide
is rushing in. My shoes already float.
I walk the bar, invisible now,
water to my thighs. The day's
turned smoky. A storm is blowing
thick from the east. I stand
a quarter mile out in the bay with
the tide rising and only this
strange buried bridge of sandbar under me,
calling across the breaking grey waves,
unsure whether I can still wade
or must swim against the tide to the boat
dragging its anchor loose.

Unknown territory. Strange bottom.
I live on bridges that may or may
not be there under the breaking
water deepening. I never know
what I'll step on. I never know

whether I'll make it before dark,
before the storm catches me,
before the tide sweeps me out.
The neat white houses across the bay
are fading as the air thickens.
People in couples, in boxes, in clear
expectations of class and role
and income, I deserve no pity
shivering here as the water rushes past.
I find more than clams out on
the bar. It's not my sailboat
ever, but it's my choice.

The rose and the eagle

1.

A bottle of 1961 Château Ausone
bought as soon as it was off
the boat, hard as slate
and black as
the darkest tulip
Queen of the Night,
has aged like me.
Carted from apartment
to flat, Boston,
Brooklyn, Manhattan and now
Cape Cod; in '61
I met the first
of the people I now
live with, had just
written the first poems
still serviceable.
In '64 when I bought
it the war had begun
to inhabit me
like a wandering
cancer, and as some
parts of me died
the rest toughened.

2.

Ausonius planted that vineyard
in the windy twilight of what
he would not have hesitated

to call his civilization.
He grew Paestum roses, pink and fragrant.
A passion for roses
is sensual but disciplined.
I bear scars on my arms
equably, even with pride like
the men of Trobriand who boasted
how they pleased women
in scratches across their backs.

Ausonius wrote too of cabbages
fat and cozy and grapes, walked
in his own trim garden
in the bright thrumming
dawn of summer when
roses croon scent, when
I see what tall lilies
raise chalices. I rub
my face into the pansies
as into my cat's flank,
my lover's belly. I go
with basket for picking
and pruners to shear off
the dying. Between
hard fingers I pinch
bronze Japanese beetles
humping in chewed petals.
I nip the tender wax beans.
The gardener's passion
is greedy as teeth
grinding the milky corn,

tender as fingers pressing
moist earth on the seed:
order and fecundity.

He savored friendship
on his palate, his heart rose
and flowed from his throat
to his students' opening
faces. From 1967 through '70
I bought no wine,
ashamed of tastes unbecoming
a guerrilla. I taught nothing
to anyone but studied
war in the streets and my garden
grew moles and tracts.
Justice held me by the hair
burning.

3.

Paulinus was his best
student, that fully voiced
friendship across a gap
of years that made him feel
the other as much heir
as comrade, eager to see
himself surpassed and die first.

Then Paulinus converted, put
off his body like a worn
overcoat, gave away

the family lands,
turned his wife to sister
and headed for dusty
Spain without saying goodbye.

Ausonius was sort
of Christian, dogma balanced
in the questing mind,
a bit of a pagan, he would have
enjoyed Buddhism too, hefting
it, turning it in the fine
light that ripens grapes
till they die into wine.

Paulinus saw visions seized,
smitten with light. An eagle
grasped him by the scruff
of the neck till he hung
shuddering in the streaming
icy wind five miles high:
his eyes smoked with seeing
the children swollen bagpipes
hunger played, the officers
trading men like dinner parties,
the moan of slaves thickening
over the tawdry glitter
peeling in long strips,
the power flip at the center
that cost ten years of poleaxed
corpses in the provinces,
beggars' bones still

scrabbling to be free.
Paulinus saw, and the eagle's
cry tore his throat.
The eagle's wings poked
through his back and lifted
him and he soared straight
beating into the jaws of the sun.

Truth is a master that
drives nails in the skull,
shoulds and musts zinging
like wasps, the strictness
of failure under bare feet
like shards of glass.
He went down simple as a hawk
'into a rabbit, plummeting
into must and Spain,
his poetry even improved,
and he became a saint.
Saints have no friends
except history and the force
they serve hollowing them
to bone flutes, to great
bronze bells that hang
to toll alarm and death,
to ring in the new morning
clouded and gusty.

Ausonius begged, mocked,
pleaded in graceful vessels

of his longing like Chinese vases
that broke against church walls.

Soar where I do, Paulinus
called, up here where the eye
grasps miles of pain and squalor,
of greed and power like a map
and the way through, there,
the high rocky pass
where the wind tears you
to your simple bones.

He does not return, Ausonius
said and turned his face
to the wall to die. He
does not return.

4.

Crimson roses and red causes,
savoy cabbage and grand juries:
both write poems through
me, and I am most
Ausonius with organizers,
Paulinus with litterateurs,
wanting to do two-handed justice
to the cartels of hunger, to the scent
of squat sweet strawberries ripening,

the blood of the vine
and the blood of the people.

I sat with you at the rough
table, spool from laying
phone lines, and we poked words.
Disapproval leaked from you
deadly as carbon monoxide
till I choked.
You mind my avid pleasures,
how much I invest of myself
in what you call
the private sector, and I
chafe at the committee-blocked line,
the Leninist mouthing of cadre,
the willful hoisting of an inturned
elite. I sat hiding
the week inside I had
just spent making love and friendship
and talk passionate
as either with a man
of whom you would not approve,
his voice curling in my ears,
my juices still running.
Each word I could say
would harden your nose.

You break yourself
off at the waist,

hack loose from blood roots,
bite at your own entrails.
I am the baby I was screaming
into the dark, I am the child
who sucked her finger,
I am the gang brat, I am
the woman who loved
every woman and man
I have loved, I am
the body I put on the line,
the organizer, the woman
who says nothing on the phone,
I am the woman who fights,
I am the woman who
grows roses, I am the woman
on whose tongue this one
precious glass of Château
Ausone glows like a velvet
coal, I am the friend
you turn from
who cannot be used now.
You want only half
of me and I,
I want to be whole.

FALL

Athena in the front lines

Only accidents preserve.
Athena Promachos, warrior goddess thirty feet tall,
no longer exists. Phidias
made her between wars in ruins
of a fort that had not kept the enemy out.
Making is an attack too, on bronze, on air, on time.
Sailors out on the Argo-Saronic
of gull and dolphin and bone-dry island
could see the sunlight creaking on her helmet.
A thousand years she stood over fire and mud,
then hauled as booty to Constantinople,
where the Crusaders, bouncy legionnaires
on the town, melted her down for coins.

These words are pebbles
sucked from mouth to mouth since Chaucer.
I don't believe the Etruscans or the Mayans
lacked poets, only victories.
Manuscripts under glass, women's quilts packed away
lie in the attics of museums sealed from the streets
where the tactical police are clubbing the welfare mothers.
There are no cameras, so it is not real.

Wring the stones of the hillside
for the lost plays of Sophocles they heard.
Art is nonaccident. Like love, it is
a willed tension up through the mind
balancing thrust and inertia, energy

stored in a bulb. Then the golden
trumpet of the narcissus pokes up
willfully into the sun, focusing the world.

The epigraphs stabbed the Song of Songs
through the smoking heart (The Church
Prepares for Her Bridegroom). The seven hundred thousand
four hundred and fifty second tourist stared
the Venus de Milo into a brassiere ad.
Generations of women wrote poems and hid
them in drawers, because an able
woman is a bad woman. They expired
leaking radioactivity among pastel underwear.

A woman scribbling for no one doodles,
dabbles in madness, dribbles shame.
Art requires a plaza in the mind, a space
lit by the sun of regard. That tension
between maker and audience, that feedback,
that force field of interest, sustains
an I less guilty than Ego, who can utter
the truths of vision and nightmare,
the truths that spill like raw egg from the
cracking of body on body, the thousand
soft and slimy names of death, the songs
of the blind fish that swim
the caverns of bone, the songs
of the hawks who soar and stoop grappling

and screaming through the crystalline
skies of the forehead.

Though the cod stifle in the seas, though
the rivers thicken to shit, still
writing implies faith in someone listening,
different in content but not in need
from the child who cries in the night.

Making is an attack on dying, on chaos,
on blind inertia, on the second law
of thermodynamics, on indifference, on cold,
on contempt, on the silence
that does not follow the chord resolved,
the sentence spoken, but the something
that cannot be said. Perhaps there are no
words yet, perhaps the words bend the thought
back on itself, perhaps the words can be said
but cannot yet be heard, and so
the saying arches through the air and crumbles.

Making is an act, but survival
is luck, caught in history
like a moth trapped in the subway.
There is nothing to do but make well,
finish, and let go. Words
live, words die
in the mouths of everybody.

The summer invasion, and the fall

We liked her especially
because she was the color of sand
blending better with Cape grasses
than other ring-necked pheasants.
Today a hunter fired close by.

How I hate it every year
when the state releases them.
When the last of the summer traffic
has dwindled honking, when the fields
look clean again, they pick their way
with proud gait through the
bayberries, their soft plumage
dazzling, broad in the beam
as galleons under sail: how
pleased they are to be free.
They strut with the mourning
doves, the bluejays, the white
throated sparrows to the food
we put down. They do not know
they are exotica for hunters
to blow holes in. For a year
and a half we protected a pair.
The male had us trained
to feed them on demand. Ker-awk,

Ker-awk, he would summon us,
gargling gravel in his steeple neck.

A man came out of the marsh,
tore down the signs as he went
and shot the female in our yard.
We were glad the male seemed
to have escaped till we met
him on the road with his
leg shot off, flying
in crooked circles.

By October the summer tourist
garbage has sunk into the bushes. The Disney
puppies, the cuddly kittens
they got for their children like soft
icecream cones to consume
have been thrown away pregnant,
starving. The cats haunt the narrow
lanes of Provincetown. I find
their ribbed hulks by the road.
The dogs run in packs on the beach
warring with seagulls. Few

go wild successfully, animals
disposed of like used paper plates
after a picnic.

In November come beer cans heaped under
the oaks, spent shells, the brown trails
of deer with arrows in their bellies,
by the ponds the pellets of lead
the ducks will eat: the vermilion
hunters, national guardians
of a male mystique.

They polish their cars and campers;
do not dent them if you wish to live,
the tourists, the hunters. They oil
their lawn mowers at home, they
clean their shotguns and carry electric
knives, canopeners, blankets, chairs,
vibrators. They photograph the ocean
and drop plastic bottles in.
If something moves beautifully
through the grass it must be
bought in a package
raped, or shot.

Crows

They give me a bad
reputation, those swart rowers
through the air, heavy winged
and heavy voiced, brass tipped.
Before us they lived here
in the tallest pine. Shortly
after coming I walked in
on a ceremony, the crows
were singing secretly
and beautifully a ritual.
They divebombed me. To make
peace I brought a sacrifice,
the remains of a leg
of lamb. Since then
we have had truce.
Smart, ancient, rowdy and far-
sighted, they use our land
as sanctuary for raiding
where men shoot at them.

They come down, settling like
unwieldy cargo jets, to the bird
food, scattering the

cardinals, the juncos. *God*
they're big, I've never seen
them so near a house,
the guest says. We look
at each other, the crows
and me. Outside
they allow my slow approach.
They do not touch our crops
even in the far garden
in the bottomland. I'm aware
women have been burned
for less. I stand
under the oldest white oak
whose arms coil fat as pythons
and scream at the hunters
driving them back
with black hair coarse and streaming:
Caw! Caw!

What looks back

Out through the pores she
is leaking slowly
while she sleeps and from
the bathroom mirror in the morning
how they yawn,
sucking mouths of babies,
gaping mouths of nestlings,
feed me!

Tracks in the dunegrass,
ripple of snake belly,
tictac of mouse foot,
zigzag of rabbit hopping.
The flesh is drying
into sand blowing.
The sand is hardening
into gravel, the silt
builds in her throat.
Cataracts of despair
grey her eyes.

The mirror is a pit
more caustic than lye.
Its calculating scan
prices the flesh.
Only the young smile at it.
To them it makes glass promises

on which to cut the fingers
and the throat.
On its pale slate damage
is figured, the erosion
of pain, the cost of laughter.

On its ice the eyes skate
meeting themselves
with a shudder, mating
like parameciums, exchanging
some of each substance,
some blood on the mirror,
some ice in the blood.

The quiet fog

The pitch pines fade
into a whiteness
that has blotted the marsh.

Beyond
starts ten feet
outside the magic circle
of lit house.

The hill has dissolved.
The road ends
under a soft wall
that creeps.

Why am I happy?
I cradle my elbows
corners of a mirror
tall as childhood
reflecting
nothing.

At the core

Quiet setting the rough hairy roots
into the hole, tamping the compost;
quiet cutting the chicken between
the bones, so the knife
rarely needs sharpening as it
senses the way through;
quiet in the hollow setting
the feet down carefully so the quail
bow their heads and go on pecking;
silence as my cats walk round
and round me in bed butting
and kneading my chest with their
sharp morning feet;
silence of body on body until
the knot of the self loosens gushing;
my living is words placed end to end,
oddly assorted cuneiform bricks
half broken, crumbling, sharp,
just baked with shiny sides
and raw edges. Even in sleep
words clatter through my head
roughly, like a wheelbarrow of
bricks dumped out. Words are my work,
my tools, my weapons, my follies,
my posterity, my faith.
Yet when I grasp myself I find
the coarse black hair
and warm slowly heaving flank
of silence digging with strong
nailed feet its burrow
in the tongueless earth.

Ghosts

The skin falls like leaves
in slow motion, I know it,
is sifted and shifted
by the wind like a dune.
The skin that knew you
seven years back
has sluffed and grown part
of another, a Jersey cow,
an oak tree, a crow.

The years wear holes in us;
what looks solid as sheet
metal, one morning the glass
face of the next building
peers through. Theories, rhetoric
fade like a Mail Pouch ad
on an old barn, but the structure
stands firm while the winds
howl through the necessary cracks.

What lives of the woman who
loved you? The fears that twittered
stripping me bare and bony
have risen in a shrill flock
and settled in younger women.
I worry about money
but rarely about my face;

responsibilities hang at my tits
squealing and fat as baby pigs.

Your ghost curls floating in the closed
waters of dream. Your mouth
moves on my throat in the dark,
my hands exactly form your back,
unscalded by the blood of our parting.
I wake trembling in a body you never
touched, while past the curve of the earth
you sleep. Time thickens you.
On the street would I know your face?

If they come in the night

Long ago on a night of danger and vigil
a friend said, *Why are you happy?*
He explained (we lay together
on a hard cold floor) what prison
meant because he had done
time, and I talked of the death
of friends. *Why are you happy
then* he asked, close to
angry.

I said, I like my life. If I
have to give it back, if they
take it from me, let me only
not feel I wasted any, let me
not feel I forgot to love anyone
I meant to love, that I forgot
to give what I held in my hands,
that I forgot to do some little
piece of the work that wanted
to come through.

Sun and moonshine, starshine,
the muted grey light off the waters
of the bay at night, the white
light of the fog stealing in,

the first spears of the morning,
how beautiful touching a face
I love. We all lose
everything. We lose
ourselves. We are lost.

Only what we manage to do
lasts, what love sculps from us;
but what I count, my rubies, my
children, are those moments
wide open when I know clearly
who I am, who you are, what we
do, a marigold, an oakleaf, a meteor,
with all my senses hungry and filled
at once like a pitcher with light.

The root canal

You see before you an icing of skin,
a scum of flesh
narrowly wrapped around a tooth.
This too is red as a lion's
heart and it throbs.
This tooth is hollowed out to a cave
big enough for tourists
to go through in parties with guides
in flat-bottomed boats.
This tooth sings opera all night
like a Russian basso profundo.
This tooth plays itself like an organ
in an old movie palace; it is
the chief villain, Sidney Greenstreet,
and its laughter tickles with menace.
This tooth is dying, dying
like a cruel pharaoh, like a
fat gouty old tyrant assembling
his wives and his cabinet, his horse
and his generals, his dancing girls
and his hunting cheetah, all
to be burned on his tomb
in homage. I am nothing,
nothing at all, but a reluctant
pyramid standing here, a grandiose
talking headstone for my tooth.

How I weave trouble

I am happy at the typewriter,
happy hilling up the soil
at the base of the spindly young leeks,
happy walking the dune road
watching for plover, happy
rolling wine on my tongue,
happy stirring the thick soup.

When I complicate my life
why do I smile,
smile as if I had just
crushed a fat sweet
oyster against my teeth?

When an old lover springs
up again like an amanita mushroom
beside my path, when a
new lover coalesces from
the glittering cloud of a party,
when I begin to balance
lunches and suppers and
afternoons and evenings
and whole nights through

like a pile of too many
plates on a tray, why
do I smile?

An urge to elaboration
like the genius of Oriental
carpets grips me. I want
borders inside borders,
medallions and intricate mosaics
of thread. You could say
I was weaned from the rich
breast milk too young, you
could say I was starved of
love and am its glutton. You
could say I like to have
many houses where I am welcomed
in, many hidey holes, many
beds where I can curl
and be warmed. You could say
when I travel I want to

be met, when I come home
I want to be greeted.
I sniff like a cat at
new boxes and hop in.

You could say love leaps burning
hot in me like the fires
of a star and it needs many
windows, many doors, or it eats
me to ash. Energy forces me
outward expanding like a universe
yet I can stand to leave
nothing, no one I have loved.

So I weave back and
forth, forth and back,
a rug patterned of warmth
and light, and when I find
a new scarlet thread shining
to add to the design,
I smile.

Sutter's Gold and the rainbow's end

Two days past I picked a salmon bud
off the Sutter's Gold. The rose
has opened full and fragrant,
buttery gold in the heart,
corolla of buff,
flushed on the fat outer petals
with dark pink. It tops the spire
of twelve-sided bottle a friend dug up.
On the pale amethyst old glass turns:
A. D. Ashley's Red Sea Balsam,
New Bedford, Mass.

The bottle stands on the draft of my new novel.
Perfume seeps to my nose, tickling
my head from the inside like wine.
Always I believe I will die
before I complete the arc of work.
My blood will splash like red ink
over the highway and the words
will cool into the ground.

Always I fear as I approach the far bank
my deductions will prove faulty,
my formulas mad,
my imagination dim and dirty.
Always I believe the bridge
will fall in the river
and I will drown.

When the final draft is tacked
down with the last comma, then I try

to avoid driving, heights, depths,
sharp edges, blunt instruments, edges of the land
because opening in me
slowly like a rose of too many petals
is the desire of dying.

I may feel guilty after a poem
for what is revealed, for what
stands bare when the speaking stops,
for what utters itself with full wings spread
of angel or bat
but I am healed to the saying.
I think it must be.

Fiction wells from a different source.
Inventing characters and playing them
foul tricks, someone
must keep count for them.
The rhythms are long, like
the round cf the seasons,
the drama of searching for roots,
berries, the gathering over
the quickening growth of hunger,
the pursuit of the hunt,

the killing, the meal,
the rich hot catharsis of sex,
the seed buried like a corpse
to raise up a green shoot.
All stories end
in some kind of death.

The roses of October are precious
in their pathos, bright and fragrant
against the falling leaves.
I picked the Sutter's Gold to remind me
I may love myself a little
even when my work is done,
that many things are beautiful besides art,
that if a rosebush can sit in the frozen
earth enduring a dormant season,
maybe I can learn to work without
anxiety running its ripsaw in my throat,
to bear those peculiar paper flowers
which carry in their centers
both birth and death, let go
and live on.

In the wet

How you shine from the inside
orange as a pumpkin's belly,
your face beautiful as children's
faces when they want
at white heat, when fear pinches
them, when they have not learned
how to lie well
yet.

Your pain flows into me through
my ears and fingers. Your pain
presses in, I cannot keep it away.
Like a baby in my body
you kick me as you stretch
and knock the breath out.

Yet when I shook with pain's
fever, when fear chewed me
raw all night, you held me, you

held on. Then I was the baby
past words and blubbering.
The words, the comfort were yours
and you nurtured me shriveled
like a seed that would
never uncurl.

How strangely we mother each
other, sister and brother, lovers,
twins. For you to love me means
you must love yourself.
That is what loving is, I say,
it is not pain, it is not
pleasure, it is not compulsion
or fantasy, it is only a way
of living, wide open.

Beauty I would suffer for

Last week a doctor told me
anemic after an operation
to eat: ordered to indulgence,
given a papal dispensation to run
amok in Zabar's.
Yet I know that in
two weeks, a month I
will have in my nostrils
not the savor of rendering goosefat,
not the burnt sugar of caramel topping
the Saint-Honoré cake, not the pumpernickel
bearing up the sweet butter, the sturgeon
but again the scorched wire,
burnt rubber smell
of willpower, living
with the brakes on.

I want to pass into the boudoirs
of Rubens' women. I want to dance
graceful in my tonnage like Poussin nymphs.
Those melon bellies, those vast ripening thighs,

those featherbeds of forearms, those buttocks
placid and gross as hippopotami:
how I would bend myself
to that standard of beauty, how faithfully
I would consume waffles and sausage for breakfast
with croissants on the side, how dutifully
I would eat for supper the blackbean soup
with madeira, followed by the fish course,
the meat course, and the Bavarian cream.
Even at intervals during the day I would
suffer an occasional éclair
for the sake of appearance.

A gift of light

Grape conserve from the red Caco vine
Robert and I planted five years ago:
rooted deep in the good dark loam
of the bottomland, where centuries
have washed the topsoil from the sandy
hill of pine and oak, whose bark
shows the scabs of fire.
Once this was an orchard on a farm.
When lilacs bloom in May I can find
the cellar hole of the old house.
Once this was a village of Pamet Indians.
From shell middens I can find their campground.

From the locust outside my window the fierce
hasty October winds have stripped the delicate
grassgreen fingernails. Winter is coming early.
The birds that go are gone, the plants retreating
underground, their hope in tubers, bulb and seed.

The peaches, the tomatoes, the pears
glow like muted lanterns on their shelves. All
is put down for the winter except the root crops
still tunneling under the salt hay mulch
we gathered at the mouth of the Herring River
as the sun kippered our salty brown backs.
Even the fog that day was hot as soup.
At evening when we made love
our skin tasted of tears and leather.

This year the autumn colors are muted. Too
much rain, the winds tore the leaves loose

before they cured. Tonight I will be with Robert,
tomorrow with you. I braid my life in its
strong and muted colors and I taste my love
in me this morning like something harsh
and sweet, like raw sugarcane I chewed in Cuba,
fresh cut, oozing sap.

On those Washington avenues that resemble
emperor-sized cemeteries, vast Roman mausoleum
after mausoleum where Justice and Health
are budgeted out of existence for the many, men
who smell of good cologne are pushing pins across
maps. It is time to attack the left
again, it is time for a mopping up
operation against those of us who opposed
their wars too soon, too seriously, too long.
It is time to silence the shrill voices
of women whose demands incommode men
with harems of illpaid secretaries, men
for whom industries purr, men who buy death wholesale.
Today some are released from prison and others
are sucked in. Those who would not talk
to grand juries are boxed from the light
to grow fungus on their brains and those
who talked receive a message it is time
to talk again.

I try hard to be simple. Not in my loving
because I am never happy unless stretched.
But simple in loyalty. I try hard to remember always

to ask for whom what is done is done.
Who gets and who loses? Who pays
and who rakes off the profit? Whose
life is shortened? Whose heat
is shut off? Whose children end
shooting up or shot in the streets?

I try to remember to ask simple questions,
I try to remember to love my friends and fight
my enemies. But their faces are hidden
in the vaults of banks, their names are inscribed
on the great plains by strip mining and you can
only read the script from Mars. Their secret
wills are encoded in the computers that mind
nuclear submarines armed with the godheads
of death. They enter me in the drugs I buy
that erode my genes. They enter my blood invisible
as the Sevin in the water that flows
from the tap, as strontium 90 in milk.

You are part comrade and part enemy: you
are part guerrilla and part prison guard.
I hold you in my arms, you fight beside
Blacks in Boston, but the Pentagon
has programmed your fantasies, the Bank
of America has a lien on your love. Sometimes
you care more to control me than for winning
this lifelong war. If I am your colony

you differ only in scale from Rockefeller.
I want to trust you the way I want
to drink water when my tongue is parched
and blistered, the way I want to crouch
by a fire when I have hiked miles
through the snowy woods and my toes
are numb. I want to trust you
as much as I want to live.

Let no one doubt, no onlookers, no heirs
of our agonies, how much I have loved
what I have loved. Flying back
from Washington, I saw the air steely
bright out to the huge bell of horizon.
I leaned against the plane window, cheek
to the plastic, crooning to see the curve
of the Cape hooking out in the embrace
of the water, to see the bays, the tidal
rivers, the intricate web of marshes,
the whole body of this land like beautiful
lace, like a fraying bronze net laid
on the glittering fish belly of the sea.

I sink my hands into this hillside wrist
deep, my nails are stubby and under them
always is my own land's dirt. I bring you
this gift of grape conserve from shelves
of summer sun bottled like glowing lights

I hope we will survive free and contentious to taste,
as I bring myself, my mouth opening
to taste you, my hands that know how
to touch you, belly and back and cunt,
history and politics. I bring you trouble
like a hornet's nest in a hat
to roost on your head. I bring you
struggle and trouble and love
and a gift of grape conserve to melt
on your tongue, red and winey,
the summer sun within like soft jewels
passing and strong and sweet.